Citadel

Citadel

Martha Sprackland

First published 2020 by
Liverpool University Press
4 Cambridge Street
Liverpool
L69 7ZU

British Library Cataloguing-in-Publication data
A British Library CIP record is available

ISBN 978-1-789-62102-0 softback

Typeset by Carnegie Book Production, Lancaster
Printed and bound in Poland by Booksfactory.co.uk

fui sobre agua edificada
mis muros de fuego son

I was built on water
my walls are of fire

This book is dedicated to Roddy Lumsden

Contents

Poached Eggs on Toast   1

Beautiful Game   2

A Room in London   3

A Blow to the Head   4

Melr   5

    Green Beach   5

    Ainsdale   6

    Scarlet Pimpernel   7

    Lessons   8

    Velvet Trail   9

They Admit Each Other to the Inquisitor   10

Tooth   11

God of Larks and Buntings   13

Other People's Furniture   14

Falconry   15

Go Away and Then Come Back   17

For Letting Them into the Building   18

The Work   19

An Interruption During Dinner   20

Vitrine of Tektites and Fulgurites   21

Lullaby   23

Pimientos de Padrón   24

Cocido Madrileño   25

Anti-metre   26

Hunterian Triptych   27

Endovéllico's Hour   29

Sports Metaphor   30

Aquarium   32

Ablutions   33

'The Perfect Wife'   34

Still Life Moving   37

Assassin   38

Dappled Things   39

Juana and Martha in Therapy   40

An Entertainment of Broken Letrillas for Juana
at Seventy, Incarcerated at Tordesillas   41

Confession, in Anticipation of an Orthognathic Surgery   42

Project for Scissors, Paper and an Egg   43

Mercy   44

Acciaccatura   45

Rowan   46

Charca   47

Newcomer   48

Transcript   50

Acknowledgments   52

Note   53

Poached Eggs on Toast

Felipe is unhungry,
eats only eggs when alone,
has very pale instincts. He claims Juana
pierces and exsanguinates him.

Anyway, intention's kingly yolk
spills off the countertop.

Thus separated, they weaken,
each hollowing and reducing
on a diet of crushed shell

decalcified and brittle
deprived of sunlight
and become so thin the pulse
shows through,

throbs at the fingertip
she holds against hope to
his collarbone, his dormant blood.

Beautiful Game

The first time I was in Spain   we played
        my dad, my brother   and I   chased
the escaping ball   that ran   and   bounced
the joyful corrida of the resort   owned
by the parents of the   older boy driving   pebbles
out of the blue sky   with the heavy end   of his cue
who   miscalculated the parabola   maths way off
missed   the shot cracked
my blood firework   forehead
starring the warm orange tile
my face a bomb   my mother
swooned   in the kitchenette
and I was dragged half   conscious through time
at the end of a cord
years later   I play to eat   to win
            sharking   crisp fifties
from the pigeons that swarm the table
in La Vía Láctea
I often dream   the ballistic angles
the chock and kiss of the enamel   smudge
of sky   blue chalk   at the junction of my thumb
green felt   good   play or foul   and to
understand the geometry of those   reds and yellows
  a flag racked and ready   I take sight
lean in   look long   down the line   see
exactly where every   thing   will   go

A Room in London

What do I remember? My roommates: the sanguine one
in bed to my left, hair in a ponytail, reading Joan Didion,
and the one to my right, smaller
even than me, who held up her hand
with its abstract of blood after the misoprostol
like she had the answer to a question at school
and the nurse came over with something for the sickness.
That room was like a lighthouse, very bright, very quiet.
I could've been there several hours or several days
while my mother circled the building in her car
or ate a pastry at the café across the street –
I have never asked. I had countless mugs of sugary tea,
an ache, a ferrous tongue, and then an orderly struggling to hold
my shoulders like the handles of a pneumatic drill
as she told me urgently what I already knew –
that *it's already done   it'll be much worse for you now if you don't.*
The pattern and weight of a cotton gown, at least, in pastel blue
    and green.
Our little beds, bars of autumnal light falling through the curtains.

A Blow to the Head

Enough to knock the earth from its orbit –
O I was cracked open
god streaming like daylight into the chamber
the nausea of my elliptical swerve
towards consciousness and away again
– I retreated into the citadel –
walked quiet pathways during the bombardment
(which was habit-forming, I was fortified)
knew that beyond the wall something
was spilling, blood or yolk onto tile – I made
my way to the innermost room.
My hand was the key – found her strung
like a diver – eyes shut, calm and before
the old world dragged me back I loosed
the cord from her wrists – woke
back into a different time with the end
of it in my hand

Melr

i. Green Beach

First, my childhood's depth of field, the spirit-
level horizon in plum-grey ruling off the Irish Sea.

Ploughland and copse, water towers
stacked backwards in decreasing saturation.

On clearer days the oil rig balanced
like a waterboatman on the meniscus, distance

ironing the sea's serrations smooth.
I could send my eyes to flock and light

on Blackpool, Barrow, the tip of my family
near the northmost edge of Wales

to bring back signals from farther afield,
the cusp of a word on the land's lip.

On a cold beach walk, wind savaging waves,
I waded out into the webbing water,

back turned on the town, and listened
while my little brother lifted razors from the sand.

The weather whined along the dunes
the sea's heavy industry tearing

our mother's speech out as gull feathers
that whipped past me and raced out and away

never   mind   she's   growing up
*   shh   that's*
*   all*

ii. Ainsdale

In Domesday Einulvesdel,
Einulf's valley between sand and moss,
littoral streak of poor soil and crushed shell.
Taxed at two gelds and tenanted
by Roger of Poitou –
lord of land *inter Mersam et Ripam*
and later Lune, also of Downholland,
Toxteth, Speke – now served
by Lib Dem ward councillors
with my primary classmates' surnames.

It doesn't stir any indifferent Viking blood,
rather pricks my ear and tongue
to hear the land-words in the stations
and culs-de-sac where I played
and feel the exhilarating proof of change:

Birkidalr, birch-tree valley.
Sef-tun, sedge farmstead where rushes grow.

Meols, in place-names of my town
and place-names of towns in Iceland
as *Melar*, meaning sandbank,
the currency of the place, tamed
and sifted through the hourglass of the plant
for fine-grain building stuff and silica,
felt at the roots of my hair, in my bedsheets,
banked up in drifts against the kerbs,
under me as I lay on the beach at night.

Fornaby, with a twin, Fornebu, under Oslo Airport.
Krossabyr, village of the cross.
Euerton, who resisted the Armada.

I grew up coastal with the land to my back.

On the last train home from town
I would watch a reflected face out of time
flashing with gorse and rig-light,
the extinct and living looming out of the dark
Birkdale, Hillside, Ainsdale, Woodvale, Linacre,
Cilduuelle, Maegoehalh, Stochestede
a rhyming song for sleep that tumbled
down the coastline, over the dunes
sighing and slipping,
renaming themselves in their sleep.

iii. Scarlet Pimpernel

I worked on it the night before the village show:
A miniature arrangement of flowers,
in the drink of a spiral shell.

I, competitive and bookish lout
wanted the pimpernel
who bloomed at sunup, also called
shepherd's weather-glass, who'd shutter up
at first sign of cloud –

I think for this reason I thought it rare,
though it grew like bloodspill
along the sandblown verges of the bypass.

So on show-day he woke me up at five
and we crept out of the sleeping house
and to the pine forest's edge and quested.

Have I collapsed time to think
he shouted *Here it is!* almost as soon as we'd arrived?
Perhaps some lapse in memory accounts for it.

We snipped and damped it, wrapped it
in kitchen roll and foil (*Be careful!*)

and sped back to the house under a pinking sky
to crown my tiny bouquet with its little flame.

I can't remember, anyway, if I won the prize.
But, wait. I wonder now if it was that
he woke at *three*, and marked the place,
then came back home to wake me up at five?

iv. Lessons

You never were good at it, anyway.
Catalyst, chemical – words are little
help, a poor match, are insubstantial.

So skip the lessons for the beach,
the landscape all horizon but for
the uprights of sand-whipped post,
Gormley effigy, the trivet of the rig.

They could've explained it this way:
in these gritty fields, the bleached
shoulders of sheep scatter the ploughlines.
Even inland, a million shells are blown

from the dunes in translucent pink
and perse and striped slate light enough
to let the wind fill and take them.

Or like this, with burnt gorse and pitchy
salt-stained hands. When the boys touch lighters
to the scrub you *get* the exchange of energy
birthing that red leap of flame. This is elementary.

But above you, a white sky – nothing. And out there
the chalky flash of the sea thundering over the beach,
pouring itself endlessly from beaker to beaker
held up to the pale light to look for changes.

v. The Velvet Trail

Long games lengthened, youth's circle spreading
like a stain over the sand, casting light
on rare flora that bloomed there:

grass of parnassus, early marsh orchid,
wintergreen, dune helleborine. My friends
stepped in and out of sight between the pines,

their shadows stretching as the tide
moved in towards our feet. Or perhaps
it was we who moved towards the boundary

inexorable as the moon's new pull?
The burning stars of our cigarettes danced
like gorseflowers, we mixed screwdrivers

and kissed and spewed and fought
and couples made a form in the giving sand.
Bitter pink buds arrowed up towards the sky –

a kind of gentian called seaside centaury
that flowers as the summer sets
and cools. Beyond the hollering and bass thump

and the sound of seething water, villagers heard
the clatter of the entire migratory flock
lifting off under cover of darkness.

They Admit Each Other
to the Inquisitor

First time, we met like lightning,
our eyes full of blood, and freed our ties
so we dropped to the floor. There was distant music,
soft pool light, a tourist crooning 'Stand by your Man'
to a resort karaoke machine. We thought
this could be the visitation that our mother
wanted for us – a child saint, holy –
but when we saw us next we were older, angrier,
bending the bars of time. In the city's first invincible summer
we fevered, read the symbols, were not right.
We were eighteen and pregnant and mad.
As a mosquito we bit behind the knee, whining
Remember, speak again and itched for days.
Our bloodied face was the garnet in our crown.
We starved ourselves in protest.
When we undid the cord that tied our wrists
it bound us; something in that blow
knocked through the city walls
and through it we are talking, still.
We can't explain this. In the other rooms
men are blurred by sleep, unhearing.
We two twirl the cord, the hot night loud
and near, and we write each other back –
too difficult a task alone and one of faith.

Tooth

Like a round grey stone lodged
in the fork of a tree
the tooth sits intractably
at the far back of the mouth
between the ear and the jaw.

The mouth can't close fully,
like a freezer door;
can't crank itself open
more than a few gear-teeth's width,
enough for water through a straw.

At night it wakes up
like an eyeball, lolls sourly on the tongue
rolls against the drum
tampers with the hinge
and rubs it raw.

Nothing to do, between the shift-
change of the painkillers
but listen to my bedmate
breathing asleep and the foghorns
in the hot harbour.

All the world's cameras
are on this clamorous point:
this knot, this bole, this clot,
this breaking news, this fire,
this prisoner of war,

a sealed world seething
like a black egg
incorruptible by amoxicillin
and saline wash.
I want it out.

I go down to the dockside,
oily between the cruise ships
and Maersk containers,
to gargle palmfuls of the sea
against the hard bezoar

and its faulty magic.
I idle towards
the half-bottle of whiskey,
the red-handled relief
in the kitchen drawer,

but Ed shifts and turns against me,
skin like cotton, outside the pain,
and says through sleep –
his clean sound mouth –
Honey, are you still sore?

I can't answer
round the cobblestone,
the ship, the choke, the pliers,
the acorn cracked
and pushing through the floor.

God of Larks and Buntings

With every bite, as the thin bones and layers of fat, meat, skin and
organs compact in on themselves, there are sublime dribbles of varied
and wondrous ancient flavours: figs, Armagnac, dark flesh slightly
infused with the salty taste of my own blood as my mouth is pricked
by the sharp bones – Anthony Bourdain, on eating ortolans

In Spanish *verdón*, leaf-coloured
as its English name suggests – from *hortolan*,
'the one who tends the garden'
– like Hortaleza, the sixteenth district
near where at eighteen she let a stranger
take her to his hot house, a greedy-fingered man –
not young – with a sharp tongue who bent low
lifted the sheet over his head and sighed
deeply – with what, she couldn't tell – the trapped
perfume of Armagnac and sweat or shame
as he hid from hundreds of shining eyes – but
like a diligent gardener down on his elbows
underneath the rustling trees,
his bishoply buttocks rose beyond his white veil –
absurd and defenceless – in plain view
of all the chattering and vengeful gods
ranged along the branches.

Other People's Furniture

I did have a man once whose body disgusted me,
it's true. Marshy, overspilling, crusted.
It wasn't that he was *unwashed*, more
that his badness was showing through,
bald patches on the oily arm of an old sofa.
Still, an arrangement of satin scatter-cushions
is also an abomination.

Falconry

It is a machine for the power of extraordinary sight,
a drone, with hungry instincts at the controls,
thoughts of meat and capture.

When at twelve she launches the hawk
into the sky above the Alhambra
it is for information about heaven

corroboration of rumours.
From the hunting air she sees the land
parcelled by olive groves

and the land's end, the drawn rule
of the inquisition, and then sea.
And when she flies further

understands the townships of water
marked by shining walls,
the shipping regions

blue-blue pieces tessellating
and slowly heaving. What more is there
to be learned? Already

she can see the map of her dominions
laid out in front of her
like a game of chess,   .

the black queen in her circlet
standing in the desert
like a bolt of lightning

a rent in the air, the fire-trail
of the plummeting hawk
as she stoops to the lark

and lifts it from the air. Talons,
sky whipping away, unbelief.
Sky tilts. Eye is filmy, landscape

falling past irrelevantly. The world contracts and
Juana receives the gold-eyed spear onto her fist,
admires its elegance with the lark,

turning it over, opening
its breast and glutting the palace gardens
with all that has been learned.

Go Away and Then Come Back

When I creep back and try to greet it
the sea flinches from my hand.
I was treacherous
in my abandonment.
All the poets were falling
in love with the sea, at once, like baby turtles
and I was landlocked away.
I did and did not want to be held.
I wanted to have the wavelets reach for me.
A sandstorm dream swept through
and I left the sea to people
who were more worthy of its attentions,
who didn't burn or take it
for granted, who didn't rail
against its implacable boundary,
its strict rule. And then even when the tide
recedes and all is mostly forgiven
there is an undertow of vengeance.
Each time he comes back to me I flinch
from his hand, rise up off the bed,
would drag him down into me if I could.

For Letting Them into the Building

He keeps party hours and a constant jamboree of guests
so occupied is he with the business of dying.
Often my buzzer goes because he has found the strength
to hoist himself up and shut himself in

and the porter has gone on a break
and there is no one to let in the teams
of hypodermic wellwishers and concerned uniforms
coagulating at the downstairs door.

At night I apologise to our adjoining headboards
lined up together like children in a dormitory
like the white wings of a bird
if the body of the bird in the air were a wall.

The Work

I entered into an uneasy bargain
in which it would sit on a chair not far away,
looking out of the window
and taking important things down.

I would not move too quickly,
wouldn't come over and touch its cheek.

During a work such as this,
the building of a blue world out of nothing
from the tip of a pen, I just had
to sit very still, a grateful stone in my lung.

An Interruption During Dinner

Golden ratio in oil-trail where the wheel
flew in, spiralled on its rim and left
a path across the linen.

There it is, now, burnished platter
laid out on the table, jewelled
with the rain it brought in

and a tuft of muddy grass
torn from the front lawn
worn proudly against the insignia.

Glass still falls from the window
and fills the sink. Flashes blue.
Blue, then blue, then blue, then blue, then blue —

Vitrine of Tektites and Fulgurites

Museo Geominero del Instituto Geológico y Minero de España

capital in a silver circlet sits
on the plateau of its throne

flashing handful of dropped cutlery
the cymbal shock

september lightning
arrows sparking flint

sanction the limits
bound the umber *meseta*

from the city whose plazas
bloom sudden as desert flowers

seen from the sun's
high mourning window

vista of sloped sienna tile
azoteas orange as pine resin

in ranges all the way
to the circling sierra into which

womb burdened with a burning
stone I climbed

thirsting mountains hung
with verdigris & bellringing

and then later, fearstruck
& fevered

dreamt I found a fulgurite
hollow root of blackened glass

standing in the desert
sky's raw data

riven with inclusions
a bloom in amber

or electrum, a prophecy coded
& catalogued in sand

Lullaby

Gran Sol

   Pazzen   Iroise

                              Yeu

                                    Rochebonne

Altair   Charcot   Finisterre   Cantabrico

                      Porto

Azores   Josephine   San Vicente   Cádiz   Gibraltar

      Madeira   Casablanca

             Agadir

    Tarfaya

Canarias

Pimientos de Padrón

Os pementos de Padrón
uns pican e outros non

A plateful of dark green bullets
slick in their lake of grassy blood
and charred from the fire,

still hissing and settling, smoking,
the skin lifting and curling
studded with salt-flakes.

They were our cheap roulette – *some hot,*
others not (the capsicum is brewed
by the sudden sun at summer's edge).

We were all of us bad at decisions,
lovesick, shamed or fleeing
or brisant and in shock. The city emptied

as the madrileños boarded up
the bodegas and rippled out
towards the cooler coasts

leaving us to our own boiling ghosts,
reckless enough to hold
the dare to our mouths, fire

or sweetness spreading across the tongue
and then head to the airport
for the first flight anywhere but home.

Cocido Madrileño

It was an unexplainable hunger, like a gravel pit,
and it wouldn't go away. Sickness like a fingernail moon
around its darkness. Juana went to the bodega
and bought six tins of cocido ridged
like braziers, *Litoral* stamped in red along
the white coastline, the meats reclining
in an adoring harem of chickpeas.
Juana's faith was on the wane but pork would prove it.
Morcilla, chorizo, tocino de ibérico, panceta,
soft white lard and blood and bone and smoke
tipped over the lip and into the pit, like a body
she desperately wanted to be rid of.
This, she believed, would sate her, save her.

Anti-metre

It's had fifteen years to settle
but won't, stays
mutable as a dune.
He admonishes me
for my instability.
But it's hard to build
on shifting sand,
this lifelong syncopation
between the hemispheres of my body
two fingers snapping in free time –
or one hand clapping,
the other a fist.
A calendar carved
on whaletusk
climbs only to twenty-eight –
I couldn't count on it.
The moon can't touch me.
I envy the rhythm of other women
from my bloodless march
between distant rains.
The ship rolls. The days
won't stabilise the reeling
I feel in the core,
that takes my balance –
and just when I've
forgotten it could exist
another egg drops
like a spent coffee capsule
through the body of the machine.

Hunterian Triptych

The affinity between the Fox, Wolf, Jackal, and ſeveral varieties of the
Dog, in their external form and ſeveral of their properties, is ſo ſtriking,
that they appear to be only varieties of the ſame ſpecies.

Dr John Hunter

i.

This ghostly archive, lined with labelled jars
is full of light. Each pickled thing bleached to ivory
sleeps in a glass flask of formaldehyde, shelves of pale stars
that catalogue our strange bodies' history.

I like the cuttles and the moray coiled up like a rope
or silver birch leaves in the moonlight, and the teeth
and textbook jaws and joints of elephants and antelope,
the piano lids left off to show the working underneath

the muscles strung across the hammer of the mount,
the sprung seat of the clever skeleton and costly organs
holding to account the whole machine,
but most the disunited human hand, the marinated palm

flayed neatly, peeled to show the bone in brine –
the strange compared assembly of your hand in mine.

ii.

Black malignancies glued inside the ribcage like wasps' nests,
bubbled lungs and degraded splints of bone,
bladderwrack washed up across the breast.

Ink has spilt across the clean page of the brain
and gathered into clots like cherrystones.
Gut-silk is rot and mothy with a spreading stain.

Look through the eyepiece of the what-the-butler-saw
into the peepshow of the reconstructed soldier's nose
dilated gunshot wound and unhooked blasted jaw.

Under the microscope the blood is dilute, swims with
    infiltrates,
the glands and kidneys showing scree and stones –
the myriad fascinating ways the body breaks

or fails, or lets us down. I am a tray of fragile curios
pushed carelessly from room to room on rattling wheels.

iii.

The long-limbed foetal kangaroo is like a toy,
the baleen whale like sugarwork in peppermint white.
Ranks of failed experiments, the dreaming small
of muntjac deer and armadillo packed airtight
in sterile wombs. A wasp-sized mouse wrapped in a twin,
a crocodile still umbilical to the egg, a bird in flight
attached with wire to the false sky of the lid,
an infant snake as delicate as spooled moonlight,
the perfect dolphin worked in mother of pearl and wax.
Until this, when we crouch before a case with cut-glass sight,
our hearts alarming brashly in their own warm jars,
then bolt towards the exit and the park, the natural light.

(Nine tiny phantoms ranged by month and weight
repose inside nine matryoshka bottles of frostbite.)

Endovéllico's Hour

I woke on guard inside the lighthouse room
to an unheard running sound which fled
through black and briny air – its antic tongue
licked around the granite walls, then beckoned.

Not a blue-blue siren but a skein of talk
outside the floodlight-ring of sleep,
a piece of dream worked loose that walked
me down the cliffs to the stained-wine stones

where I found the tiny party's light spilled
onto the beach – my radio, long damaged
and anyway unplugged, the circuit cold.
I took the set and climbed back into bed

as the forecast brought the rain from Finisterre.
Must have been something there that I should hear.

Sports Metaphor

Mexican wave
the crowd goes wild lifting
to their feet as one
smooth sheet of silk
rippling out of their seats unstoppable
impulse of that
final touch which
seemed impossible at the end of that far
run up the leftfield
that strenuous effort
head down chin up legs long
as deer back straight
toes poised *en pointe* tucked in stretched
out it depends on the sport
after the pass and play
the feint and fall the
falter and stumble the
dodge and drive the give and take good
god they're trying so hard
to believe that the score
has already ticked over
the line that thick white chalk
is impassable but they do
pass part and hassle the mark
a try or a swing or a perfect perfect
perfect
landing dear god of sports most
present and most responsive god
in his forehand and her backhand and his bikewheel and
her boxing glove and their tendon and their thickened
artery and their kneecap and their early death and
their shin splint and my aorta strenuous

thing *sportif* trying harder
than the one in the Euros who *skyed it*
god of left feet my heart
which means as I learned only
today to kick it hard to chalk
it up to experience to sky it right
out of the stadium yes
up and rapture and applause   ah!

Aquarium

The tank was my escape.
Dappled dome, filter hum,
the echo and boom of electronic
voices and screaming children.

Flickering fish leapt bright
above the tunnel's vault
but the sandbar kept low,
wary. The zookeeper paused

key resting in the lock,
said *Here is what I know now*
of time, and she turned
the key which opened a panel

to reveal a red handle
which she pulled, and opened wide
the yawn of glass, towering
vast and trembling –

far away, off an English beach,
the sea dropped minutely,
pulled off the sand and
exposed a thing long-buried

but I wasn't there to see it,
was facing down a sheer wall of water
full of big-eyed creatures slowly
turning around to face me.

Ablutions

He kneels on the bathroom floor
to clip his fingernails straight into the toilet.
Imagine his bent head, the concentration, the bright
metallic snip like a speckled thrush tapping
a snail against a stone.

'The Perfect Wife'

After two paintings: Demencia de Doña Juana de Castilla
(1866) by Lorenzo Vallès and Doña Juana la Loca *(1877)*
by Francisco Pradilla, both in the Museo del Prado, and the
pamphlet La Perfecta Casada *(1583) by Fray Luis de León.*

i.

He is away, but has often been away before.
He is asleep, but not for the first time.

She knows him this way, waxy
and withholding. Every reason
to think he will push through the curtains
and stride into the antechamber
with her father's fever pooling at his feet.

Delicate, the text reads, *loveliest*,
the *tender gesture* of her finger to her lips.
But no, already he comes – the scattered flowers
have begun to wilt, and Juana
hushes the courtiers with her upheld palm –

they will insist on her jealousy,
rather than this keeping close the one
who schemes, only half-hidden
behind a veil too flimsy to restrain him.

ii.

The candle yearns into the wind
which shoves it away, as always.

She is pregnant, arms hanging by her sides, unmoved
by the cold and tedium of her friends

who have heard just about enough of Felipe
from the drunken telephone.

She writes another note: *necrophilia is an excess of love*
and then revolted holds it to the flame.

There must be a way of burning this task,
of excising his clamorous body from the world.

iii.

Sleep moves over you
like a wave across the water.

You wake against me, your long-
loved body warm with the day's deep dream

and murmur your hourly votive –
How do you want me? My arrow of travel
is towards you, the lake at my back

and the sweep of sun across
your blue and gold face
scored by determined rowboats.

iv.

Extrapolated from the thirty-first proverb
Fray Luis de León's instructional pamphlet
lays out his benevolent avuncular view
of his niece's bloodsheets.

Obsequio, obsequio, obsequio.
A woman out of the home, he writes, kindly,
is a fish plucked from the water.

To keep a wet-nurse is adulterous to the husband.
Be as sweet and as interesting as milk.

In the waiting room of the Catholic clinic
I pick up another leaflet:
Get Married and Be Submissive.

Give her the reward she deserves.
Praise her in public for what she has done.

v.

He wakes, the body wakes
nightly. What is done by day –
the ministrations of white hellebore
and gorse and wych –
take root and rouse him, reach him
in his sleep and he starts – wakes at
the blue-blue of a siren screeching
around the corner of Manor Road,
sunken music rushed by as if through a portal –
and at these times she gentles him, his body like a flame –
pinches his nostrils shut and whispers *Shh*
shh   sleep   he kicks once like a dog
slips back into his muddy dream –

Still Life Moving

For all this riotous stillness
something must move.

The lilies captive in their jar,
the bread and cheese inert as loaves of stone

next to the knife
and its cold serrated blade,

the ribbon marking off a creamy page
and the bunch of iron keys

splayed like an insect on the dark wood –
all these things must move

must slip or spill or turn to rust or mould.
In this moment, the paint drying on the world

I could believe it fixed and solid
the shadows cast by the flowers on the wall

indelible, held there by a static sun.
But not so. Already the bloom

is moving bluely over the ripe cheese,
the bread is beginning to exhale,

the lilies with their weight let drop their heads.
And any moment now

shaken by some small tremor far away
that pile of apples will slip its logic

and the whole cascading rumble of them
bounce across and off the tabletop like marbles.

Are there hands, just out of frame,
that might dart forward in time to catch them?

Assassin

butter dish in the back garden   toothbrush
taken up to an attic bedroom   a
phone charger   carried around everywhere
just in case   see also   passport   clean socks
a frog in the pool filter   transfigures
into a garlic press a close family
member might approach you with a hand
axe   a stranger with a cricket bat   in
the bathroom or terrace   or pop up beside your lawn chair
and ask you to hold the baby   the baby is small
enough to be   an object   for the purposes of the game
I carry everything I think I might need
I won't take a drink from anybody   nowhere
no how   won't touch
hands with anybody I love   no one
will take the salt at dinner   because
anything can kill them   everybody   wishes
we had   never   started playing

Dappled Things

for Louis & Felix

Why are so many born patterned –
the humbug tapir, the velvet boar,
the puma kittenish in tabby stripes
before they drop their finery
and are done up into a more sombre coat? –
as my nephews were born, both
with orchid skin, pink and cream on mauve ink-mackle
like mackerel sky at evening – settling
as the blood learned more, as they became solid –
so a knot of juvenile slow-worms
in their golden nest will writhe the go-
faster stripe from their dun flanks,
shuck it – and the pup blackbird's mottle
eventually drops and makes way for the dark
plumage – its graduation robe or city suit –
more serious, it's true – and more befitting of its age –
but with a brilliant blue and jade
still carried under the wing or eyelid –

Juana and Martha in Therapy

This is what they have learned. Their putative son
imprisons them, calls them mad, instructs
the wardens to hurt and hold them.
Some days he doesn't exist at all
and they are free to go out,
to go into the centre of town without a pram,
to read books and eat a saucer of olives.
The son is too big for a pram, surely! Is almost a man.
Time is complicated, especially at these distances.
The crackling string of this makeshift telephone
between two empty tins of cocido
stretches five centuries and is desperate to forget
but they two must stay on the line, must work together
if they are to escape and write this.
They are in the bland room
above the Pret at Bishopgate, trying to understand.
The walls of the mind are deep and moated.
They had six children in nine years. They have no children.

An Entertainment of Broken Letrillas for Juana at Seventy, Incarcerated at Tordesillas

(The Geometrician, Queen of Spain, Clouded Yellow, Thyme Plume)

The millennium was rare
a clouded yellow year
when I was turning twelve
and watched swarms of sunlight
tumbling in hectic flight
off England's chalky shelf
and vanish into the clear
blue distant stratosphere.
I gave chase and wound up here:
gold edge of a Spanish night
proving something to myself,
the millennium aware
of my clouded, callow fear.
Mariposa o polilla –
tu ala embrolla mi letrilla.

Under the wings are jewels
like silver eyes or pools
that hang from the sierra
sewn in the mountain's gown
on our long journey down
the royal ephemera
fritillaries unspooled
where we bathed and kissed
before spirits of misrule.
We regained the town
and met an altered era.
Under night's wing dreamt like fools
of false eyes in silver pools.
Mariposa o polilla –
tu ala embrolla mi letrilla.

In the dehesa copse
the holm-oak drops
its acorns for the pigs
(grazed for ibérico)
who truffle from below
on cork, quejigo, figs
and at the rowan tops
the angled moth stops
sights to the equinox
and measures off his slow
ruled line over Madrid,
miles from his home copse
far where the dehesa stops.
Mariposa o polilla –
tu ala embrolla mi letrilla.

She works with minute patience
to manufacture fragrance
in notes of heat and dust
from branches of the herb
which then her wings disturb
and spill its camphor musk
into the waiting silence
her pale and odorous trance
pervades even her absence.
This is her smoky verb
and hers alone in trust:
to weave with infinite patience
the meseta's fragrance.
Mariposa o polilla –
tu ala embrolla mi letrilla.

Confession, in Anticipation of an Orthognathic Surgery

When I went to him and sat he took
my clattering head between his hands,
thumbs deep in the fosse below my earlobes

fingertips probing my cheekbones
then retracted his hands and wiped them
privately with a disinfectant wipe.

I chewed on the little bone of shame.
He said the words: *maxilla, malar, orbit, temporal*
then poured a paper cup of water at the font. *Show me.*

I took and I drank, eyes cast out to watch him
diagnose the bad bones, bad habits, awful
suckling ratchet we both knew would not mend.

My fate set, he weighed my jaw again,
steadying my skull against his palm,
a devotion hopeless as any other.

Project for Scissors, Paper and an Egg

A ream of printer paper is a road
and scissors run along it like a racer.

Chainsaw-bifurcated tree
with fibrous heart.

She had escrituras, a little writing desk,
but she is erased from the archives. Where is Juana?

She wants to glue back together
the white halves of her breakfast eggshell

but can't match the crown-points
and the edge is too fine –

there is no fixing it. The breakfast-room is dingy
so she brings in a roll of wallpaper

a dual-carriageway, roadside trees blurring
in the chew of the pulping machine

to make more paper for the hungry scissors,
and a second boiled egg for Juana to eat

whilst snipping up a pile of letters and poems
between resolute and yellow bites.

Mercy

Night after night I must gather
tens of insects – millipedes,
stinkbugs, houseflies, moths –
and expel them. At breakfast the others
share their methods, some pressing the bugs
under the thumb until they give and smear,
their legs coming apart like dry grass,
or mashing them with a book, a glass,
the heel of a shoe. The walls are remembered
with all the little deaths. I had been trapping them
between a postcard and a cup
and ferrying them laboriously downstairs
to the outside door and flicking them into the pine-litter
to crawl back up the wall and through the screen
into my bedroom for another round.
But this morning, in a fury
I caught the shield-shaped thing in my bare hand,
its legs gyrating feebly against my fingers
and ran to the bathroom, where I threw it into the toilet.
It turned small circles,
swimming an irregular stroke
in desperate search of landfall. I watched
like the eye of a lightning god, unforgiving
as it groped at the smooth blank sides.
Only after some too-long stretch of time
did I press the flush and whirl it
benevolently down into the tank.
The last of summer is leaving. Soon
the insects will all be sleeping in the walls.
If you would just call, or write to me.

Acciaccatura

I sit across from them in the Old Church
backs to a sandstone pillar – Juana and Felipe –
her sage-green collar, his catgut smile
beyond the bows indicting heaven –
Ab alto – as inscribed above the church door
here, with the date, 1563 – I've overshot
her, as always – though closer than ever …
in that same year they laid first stone at El Escorial
(that brutal slab that blocks light
from the foothills of Monte Abantos
where I climbed and saw the curvature of time) –
the viola plucks me from my reverie – Ed's elbow
in my rib and breath at my ear. It's hard
for the music-minded to only listen –
and we watch them – their eyes closed
shuddering through the *assai* like dogs in a dream.

Rowan

Crying tree
quicken-tree
eye's delight
with dark heartwood
traveller's tree
where the devil
strung her mother up
portal-tree
through which
worlds
wild service
gatekeeper
switchboard
bitter tree
my berry
swelling on the branch
eaten through by
caterpillars
geometrician
wintermoth
clouded yellow
feathered thorn
satellite tree
beaming the news
into the screen
like a dark dagger
tree of glass
of lightning

Charca

Not the upper pool, ringed like an amphitheatre
with concrete bleachers and zinc-topped tables,
a set of rough stone steps domesticating
the clenched tiptoe down into the meltwater,

but a lower rung somewhere further
down the flow of waterfalls,
apricots thudding to the path, yellow light
pouring through the valley like pollen.

The word means *puddle*, though it is deep
and clear where the three of us strip
off our watches, sunglasses, shoes
and huddle on a jutting rock

in the roar and splash of the garganta
for the courage to jump, for the twelve seconds
it takes to numb the skin so that on hauling out,
unfelt blood pours from my foot onto the dry stone.

This scene, so vivid in its lemon-olive hues,
is more than the snapshot we capture on a phone.
That something with this unassuming name – charca –
suggesting something shallow, new,

is dark and dappled, the rock altered
by the pounding snowmelt. Something frozen
and distant starts to thaw in me
and to carve these deeper channels

into which we jump, again and again,
looked over by nothing but the mountains,
the overhanging leaves,
the lifted winter lived through and unbound.

Newcomer

Новичо́к

This is the deceptive border of the year – its crux –
it has unique qualities. It can be disguised
as a powder, as a precursor to pesticide.

The way to keep track of time is by
the new buds blaring on the branch-ends
acid-green and sleek as silk.

It's sickening, their slick fecundity,
their furtive spread. Hoist on the gold pins
of their mount, their pearl vitellus glows

as an egg someone lifts to the light
to see the hard rot twist in the radix,
hold it up in their hand carefully

between all four fingers and thumb.
It's no use worrying about it.
You pull out to come, scatter opals

flecked through with blood. I turn the radio on.
Out in the sea, covertly,
goose barnacles in hiding extrude

their secret tongues to taste the air
and see if it's *time*. In the tideline
bubbles cling, whisper *sub rosa*,

the smaller ones tangential,
timestopped mid-spray by the last of frost.
When I crack an egg into a basin

and the yolk comes carrying a little bouquet
do I whisk it in, or cup it from the albumen
with a fragment of shell? Here at the climax

the redgold sheath of winter is cracking,
shouldered aside by the green shoot,
the nucleic newcomer, and calving –

A-232's advantage here is that it will not freeze.
Novichok on the news again. Any second
the trees will discharge their spores over the city

and we won't be able to breathe at all.
They are ghosts, they are rumours and talk,
not confirmed by anything.

The chimes of Big Ben come tinny
down the wires, bringing to hand the time
of day, bulletin, rumour, and something like attar

of damask – Nevarte, *new rose*, the lab flower
of a slender sable-brush heavy-laden
that heaped pollen onto the ready stamen –

something delicate as a soap bubble
that looked at too directly will collapse.
No, we said in the papers, *No, it did not exist.*

Transcript

– if you lie so, and i lie like this we can talk like sisters. i am calling you – pick up, and stretch the green surgical thread tight –

– ah, already . . . so you are in moratalaz. i am still at the alhambra, and tonight think you must be older than me. last time we used the cuerda, rough and heavy – you took it from my wrists to string our line –

– i could barely make you out, your voice was ruptured –

– from addressing my public, yes! from feigning rapture. today, though, i felt for the first time the knife-blade of god's attention and think maybe i could be fixed –

– we might both be fixed, now –

– yes. pull the string tighter. which room is this? –

– this one. the citadel. my breasts have been leaking milk –

– then it is not so late after all. i was nursed by maria de santistevan, who would murmur *la pobrecita, pobre criaturita* as she pushed my head onto the nipple –

– there's pity in it, yes –

– so much of mothering –

– did he wake? –

– tried rowan and weather-glass and gorse and hellebore –

– i'll sing you something, and you'll sleep. tomorrow i will go falconing –

– and i will go to work and try to hold the yolk of myself together, try not to spill –

– and then? –

– and then later take the metro to the aquarium, to the sharks in their tank –

– i have seen you there. i was an old woman in tordesillas, looking into the face of the water glass they left outside my door –

– lullaby me now. i'm frightened of the storm, the blades of lightning –

– it falls as glass in the desert. do you hear me? –

– i can hear it drumming on the balcony like artillery, i feel besieged –

– the city holds. on water we were built, *amor*, though our walls are of fire –

– is that an ambulance, that blue light strafing the sea? –

– it's the rig-light. turn the radio on. do you hear me? i'll sing through it and we'll run –

– sing loud, though, over the thunder –

– *Altair   Einulvesdel   Gran Sol   Finisterre   Canarias* –

Acknowledgments

Thanks to the editors of Caught by the River, the *Guardian*, *London Review of Books*, *Magma*, *Oxford Review of Books* and *Poetry*, where some of these poems were first published. Several poems appeared first in the pamphlets *Glass As Broken Glass* and *Milk Tooth*, for which thanks are due to Rack Press and Rough Trade Books.

For looking over some of the poems at various points, thanks to Andrew Parkes, Chrissy Williams, Dai George, Declan Ryan, Dimiter Kenarov, Ed Wall, Emily Hasler, Ishion Hutchinson, Jean Sprackland, Joan Fleming, Joey Connolly, Jorge Nicolás Lucini Serrano de Haro, Juan Ángel Mengual, Matthew Hollis, Matthew Marland, Nina Hervé, Patrick Davidson Roberts, Toby Martinez de las Rivas, Will Barrett. Thanks to my editor, Deryn Rees-Jones, for her patience and good sense, and for pushing me when I needed pushing.

I am grateful for time, or space, or money, or all three, to: Arvon, Arts Council England, Poetry School, Poetry Society, the Corporation of Yaddo, Maria on Calle del Desengaño, Linda Marland, Jean Sprackland & Nigel Pantling, Joan Fleming & Dom Czapla. Special thanks to Terry Craven & Charlotte Delattre and all at Desperate Literature, including the whole *La Errante* gang, for being a home.

Thanks to all my family, on all sides. And to the delinquents, for endless entertainment.

With love to Ed Lake, and to Juana de Castilla.

Note

The epigraph to the book is from the twelfth-century motto of the city of Madrid: *fui sobre agua edificada, mis muros de fuego son, esta es mi insignia y blasón* ('on water I was built, my walls are made of fire, this is my flag and coat of arms'). Madrid's first name, when it was settled in the ninth century, was Mayrīt, an Arabic word meaning 'many springs', a reference to the rivers and underground streams that came together. The citadel walls were built of local flint, and during the many great sieges the metal arrowheads and spears striking against the stone would send sparks, giving the impression the city was burning. If you take a coin to the Plaza de la Villa and strike it, surreptitiously, against the walls of the Casa Cisneros, near where I lived in La Latina, you can send a spark from that flint.